100 Powerful Prayers for Your Teenagers.

Scriptural Promises and Prayers to Let God Take Control of Your Teenagers. Get Them to Experience Love & Fulfillment

70 Powerful Promises of God to Believe for Your Teenagers and 70 Prayers to Let God Take Control of Their Lives in Different Situations.

Katie Armstrong

Disclaimer

The information presented herein represents the views of the author as of the date of publication. Because of the rate with which conditions change, the author reserves the rights to alter and update her opinions based on the new conditions. This product is for informational purposes only and the author does not accept any responsibilities for any liabilities resulting from the use of this information.

While every attempt has been made to verify the information provided here, the author and her referrals cannot assume any responsibility for errors, inaccuracies or omissions. Any slights of people or organizations are unintentional.

Copyright © August 2016 by Katie Armstrong

All Rights Reserved. Contents of this book may not be reproduced in any way or by any means without written consent of the publisher, with exception of brief excerpts in critical reviews and articles.

Published By:

Better Life Media.

BETTER LIFE WORLD OUTREACH CENTER.

Website: www.BetterLifeWorld.org

Email: info@betterlifeworld.org

Any scripture quotation in this book is taken from the KJV except where stated. Used by permission.

All texts, calls, letters, testimonies and enquiries are welcome.

Contents.

Disclaimer...3

Introduction...7

Chapter One: 6 Strong Reasons & Benefits of Praying For Your Teenage Children Every Day...12

Chapter Two: Getting Started With Praying For Your Children...24

Chapter Three: How to Pray For Teenage Children Using the Prayers in This Book....31

Chapter Four: Salvation Prayers for Children....33

Chapter Five: Healing Prayers....42

Chapter Six: Prayers for Academic Excellence....52

Chapter Seven: Praying for the Prodigal, Disobedient Teen....61

Chapter Eight: Prayers to Drive Away Fear, Discouragement and Depression in Children....69

Chapter Nine: Prayers for Guidance in Choosing Career and in Relationship....79

Chapter Ten: Prayers for Protection....88

Chapter Eleven: General Prayers and Declarations For Your Children....94

Contact Us....102

About the Author....103

Introduction.

As children grow and mature, it's almost like parents have to learn how to be a parent all over again, because nurturing youngsters is a completely different practice from nurturing the very same children through their earlier childhood and junior school years.

Teenagers stand with one foot in childhood and one foot in adulthood, so there is a very careful harmonizing act that parents must master in order to foster the present and future success of their child. This balance art of raising your teenagers is a major subject that most parenting books and websites are trying to teach parents.

But I wholeheartedly believe that an earnest heartfelt prayer strategy for your child is a major factor that will take care of what most strategies will not achieve.

God has shown me that there are things we may not be able to do for our children. But when we pray for them every day and speak God's word over their lives, we get God committed in their pursuits. When God works in their lives, He teaches and helps them across so many things, more than we could have done by just trying.

THANK YOU FOR ORDERING THIS BOOK.

Please consider giving this book a review on Amazon.

Also, please help us spread the gospel to the hinterlands of Africa and Asia by checking out our other titles and purchasing them for yourself and loved ones. These titles will surely bring blessings to your life and family.

1. <u>200 Violent Prayers</u> for Deliverance, Healing and Financial Breakthrough.

2. <u>GRIEF AND LOSS:</u> Hearing God's Voice in Painful Moments: 21 Days Bible Meditations and Prayers to Bring Comfort, Strength and Healing When Grieving for the Loss of Someone You Love.

3 . <u>Healing Prayers:</u> 30 Powerful Prophetic Prayers that Brings Healing and Empower You to Walk in Divine Health.

4. Healing WORDS: 55 Powerful Daily Confessions & Declarations to Activate Your Healing & Walk in Divine Health: Strong Decrees That Invoke Healing for You & Your Loved Ones

5. Prayers That Break Curses and Spells and Release Favors and Breakthroughs.

6. 7 Days Fasting With 120 Powerful Night Prayers for Personal Deliverance and Breakthrough.

7. 100 Powerful Prayers for Teenagers

8. How to Pray for Your Children Every Day.

9. How to Pray for Your Family: + 70 Powerful Prayers and Prophetic Declarations for Your Family's Salvation, Healing, Victory, Breakthrough & Total Restoration.

10. <u>Daily Prayer Guide:</u> A Practical Guide to Praying and Getting Results – Learn How to Develop a Powerful Personal Prayer Life

11. <u>Make Him Respect You:</u> 31 Relationship Advice for Women to Make their Men Respect Them.

12. <u>How to Cleanse Your Home and Property from Demonic Attacks</u>

13. <u>Praying Through the Book of Psalms:</u> Discover Great Psalms, Powerful Prayers & Declarations for Every Situation: Birthday, Christmas, Business Ideas, Breakthrough, Deliverance, Healing, Comfort, Exams, Decision Making, Grief, and Many More.

Chapter One: 6 Strong Reasons & Benefits to Pray For Your Teenage Children Every Day.

---

1. Your Children Are the Gifts From God.

Behold, children are a gift of the LORD, The fruit of the womb is a reward.

Like arrows in the hand of a warrior, So are the children of one's youth.

Psalm 127:3-4

You may love your child so much, but the truth remains that God is the one who actually gave you that child. You cannot love your child more than God who created them.

When you pray for your children with the Word of God you are simply turning them over to the creator who gave them to you and asking Him to direct them and enable them to become what He made them to be.

---

2. God Wants Your Children To Be Saved And Blessed.

Then children were brought to him that he might lay his hands on them and pray. The disciples rebuked the people.

but Jesus said, "Let the little children come to me and do not hinder them, for to such belongs the kingdom of heaven."

And he laid his hands on them and went away.

Matthew 19:13-15

Two things are obvious in this scripture.

1. *God wants children to be saved from sin and the power of Satan.*
2. *He wants to bless them so they can have a great life here on earth and fulfill their destinies.*

However, we must make conscious efforts to bring the children to Him. We must not allow religion, education and modernization to hinder us from taking them to God and seeking His blessings.

The disciples in the above story represent everything that looks good, like education, religious activities, computer and so on. These things will try to stop us from taking our children to God. But we must say no. There is no alternative to God's blessings on our children.

Their computer knowledge and education cannot guarantee a great life. We must pray for our children.

---

3. Praying For Your Children Is One Of The Best Ways To Use The Rod Of Correction.

The Bible says that:

He who withholds his rod hates his son, But he who loves him disciplines him diligently - **Proverbs 13:24**

Foolishness is bound up in the heart of a child; The rod of discipline will remove it far from him. - **Proverbs 22:15;**

There's a public disagreement as to the meaning of rod in that scripture. While some people say that spanking a child as a correction strategy is a must, others disagree completely and recommend we search for the meaning of that scripture elsewhere.

I don't think there's anything wrong with spanking a child with love. But much more than that is that <u>rod in the Bible signifies the Word of God.</u>

Even though I walk through the valley of the shadow of death, I fear no evil, for You are with me; **Your rod and Your staff, they comfort me.** - Psalm 23:4

God's Word is the ultimate rod of correction, deliverance, comfort and judgment on the enemies. Don't spare the use of this rod over your children. Learn to pray and confess the Word over them, for their complete wellbeing. That is the most effective use of the rod of correction.

---

4. So That They Can Fulfill God's Plans for Their Lives.

The best use of life is living in the reality of knowing that we are doing God's will. That's the only way to have peace and be free from the chaos and intense pressures that this life presents.

> *"These things I have spoken unto you, that in me ye might have peace. In the world ye shall have tribulation...-* John 16:33

Praying the Word of God over our teenage children will empower them spiritually to learn about God's ways and fulfill His plans for their lives.

Don't worry if it seems you have prayed for your children for a long time, yet it seems they are still far from coming to the reality of God's love and salvation.

The Word never fails. It is working. Keep praying, confessing and believing. Your prayers are producing   fruits.

---

5. Praying For Your Children Is A Good Inheritance to Bequeath to Them.

"A good man leaveth an inheritance to his children's children: and the wealth of the sinner is laid up for the just."

Proverbs 13:22

Love and care, Business, wealth and education are great gifts we can leave for our children, but of greater value is the gift of prayer for them.

How great it feels when children look back and say:

"My mom always prayed for me. She never missed that. I owe her a lot."

"My dad would bless me and pray always and tell me that God is with me. That I won't get lost"

There is no inheritance greater than that gift of eternal love.

Let us start giving it regularly today and refuse to be discouraged by the look of things as they appear to be at the moment. Prayer works, both now and later.

6. To Stop Satan's Attacks on Them.

"Be sober, be vigilant; because your adversary the devil, as a roaring lion, walketh about, seeking whom he may devour:"

1 Peter 5:8

Satan is after your children.

Just imagine the way our schools and social media are filled with all sorts of vulgar words, violence, graphic images and wrong teachings in the name of liberalization. Satan has filled the society with false theories on abortion, sex, afterlife, church and so on.

He has turned our public schools into cesspits of godless propaganda where God is publicly mocked and reviled. The ultimate end is to get them busy with all sorts of nonsense, and then ruin the family and society.

There are two reasons he wants our children:

First, as evidenced by the passage above, Satan wants to destroy the lives of anyone he can attack, and children being generally more susceptible than adults, are a primary target of his schemes.

Second, he believes if he gets your children, it will be easier for him to get you (for evidence, see Job 1:18-19), and he wants you, too.

Fortunately, we are not left helpless against such a potent adversary. God has given us power to resist the devil over our children and family through prayer and His Word.

Chapter Two: Getting Started With Praying For Your Children.

There's so much that the devil is doing to target your children. It's a big situation that calls for urgent attention. Let us, as parents take up the responsibility of praying for them daily. The Bible says:

> "The rod and reproof give wisdom: but a child left to himself bringeth his mother to shame."
>
> **Proverbs 29:15:**

> And they brought young children to him, that he should touch them: and his disciples rebuked those that brought them.

But when Jesus saw it, he was much displeased, and said unto them, Suffer the little children to come unto me, and forbid them not: for of such is the kingdom of God.

Verily I say unto you, Whosoever shall not receive the kingdom of God as a little child, he shall not enter therein.

And he took them up in his arms, put his hands upon them, and blessed them.

Mark 10: 13-16

The rod of reproof is the Word of God. The best way to use it is to stand in the gap and use it to claim your children for the Almighty God in prayers.

In these days and times that our teenage children face even more challenges than we can talk about, it's very important that we pray every day for them. Just take a look at some of the threats that your children face the moment they leave your house every day, which they must overcome:

- Violence through Indoctrination.
- Prostitution
- Internet Pornography.
- Bullying
- Peer pressure
- Graphic images

- Social media attacks
- Abortion
- Hate
- Diseases and spiritual attacks.

As a parent, you need to listen to the urgent call to start praying for your children today. To get started, you need to:

---

1. Accept The Call to Pray for Your Children.

> *"Today when you hear his voice, don't harden your hearts as Israel did when they rebelled."*
>
> **-Hebrews 3:15 (NLT)**

It is God who is asking you to bridge the gap and be a part of history by praying and confessing God's Word on your children and those you can gain access to. Every little act of righteousness is a seed that produces everlasting results. Your prayers can save, heal, protect and achieve more results than other parenting ideas could achieve.

---

2. Ask God For Grace.

"For by grace are ye saved through faith; and that not of yourselves: it is the gift of God:"

- Ephesians 2:8

Say this prayer:

"Oh LORD, I accept Your call. I know You love my children even more than I do. They are the stories of our tomorrow. Father, give me grace to pray, speak Your Word and walk with You in all issues regarding my children henceforth. In Jesus name."

---

3. Believe Your Prayers.

Before you start praying, believe that when you pray, God will answer. Your prayer will produce great results and cause great changes to happen.

> *Therefore I tell you, whatever you ask for in prayer, believe that you have received it, and it will be yours.* **– Mark 11:24 (NIV)**

> *If you believe, you will receive whatever you ask for in prayer."* – **Matthew 21:22 (NIV)**

Your prayer will move mountains. Don't let the devil discourage you that you are just wasting your time. We are not going to be worried with physical situations as they appear to be.

We are seeing our children respond to the LORD and fulfill the plan of God for their lives. We are seeing them take right decisions and influence their environments positively. We are seeing them resist temptations and speak up for justice. That is what is happening as we pray.

Chapter Three: How to Pray For Your Children Using the Prayers in This Book.

---

1. Our goal is to pray the scriptures:

We'll use the WORD of God in every case to pray. Praying the WORD of God is more effective than praying our own words.

For example, when praying for a child's salvation, you'll take God's WORDS in several places like the one in John 6:44 and pray thus:

> *O LORD, "No one can come to Christ unless the Father draws them. Therefor Father, I ask that You draw Mike to the knowledge of Christ in Jesus name*

By praying the scriptures over our children severally, we'll invoke the Will of God in their lives because the Word of God is Yea and Amen.

2. Being specific is always very good.

In the dashes in each prayer point, put the name of your child or the children you are praying for.

Pray with fervency and be persistent. God answers prayers.

Chapter Four: Salvation Prayers for Children.

God's Promises:

1.

"Even so it is not the will of your Father who is in heaven that one of these little ones should perish." - **Mattew 18:14**

2.

"The Lord is not slack concerning His promise, as some count slackness, but is longsuffering toward

us, not willing that any should perish but that all should come to repentance." - **2 Peter 3:9**

3.

"This is good, and pleases God our Savior, who wants all people to be saved and to come to knowledge of the truth." - **1 Timothy 2:3-4**

4.

"Believe in the Lord Jesus and you will be saved, along with everyone in your household." - **Acts 16:31.**

5.

Then Jesus said to them, "Suppose you have a friend, and you go to him at midnight and say, 'Friend, lend me three loaves of bread; a friend of mine on a journey has come to me, and I have no food to offer him.'

And suppose the one inside answers, 'Don't bother me. The door is already locked, and my children and I are in bed. I can't get up and give you anything.'

I tell you, even though he will not get up and give you the bread because of friendship, yet because of your shameless audacity[a] he will surely get up and give you as much as you need.

"So I say to you: Ask and it will be given to you; seek and you will find; knock and the door will be opened to you.

For everyone who asks receives; the one who seeks finds; and to the one who knocks, the door will be opened. **- Luke 11:5-10 (NIV)**

Prayers & Declarations:

1.

Thank You LORD, because you do not want my children to perish. Thank you LORD because you want me and my household to be saved. This is the assurance I have in YOU that as I pray, I receive answers. In Jesus name.

2.

LORD I declare that my children shall be saved and come the knowledge of the truth in Christ Jesus. Let Your power of salvation visit them ---------------

------*wherever they are right now. Visit them right now in the name of Jesus Christ.*

3.

O LORD my Father, I fall to my knees before You and ask that out of Your indefinite resources, You will empower _____ with inner strength to accept Jesus as Lord and savior. In Jesus name.

4.

"Cause _____ to be planted deep in the Love of Christ. Let him be rooted deep in Your love and

comprehend with all of God's people the extravagant dimensions of Your love. In Jesus name.

5.

"I come against the spirit of rebellion in the life of -- --------------in Jesus name. I cast out every spirit of stubbornness and rebellion; I command these anti-salvation spirits to be drown in the abyss in the Mighty name of Jesus Christ.

6.

Satan, lose your grips on -------------------------- right now in Jesus name.

7.

Jesus sets you----------------- free, you are therefore free indeed. You are no longer under the influence of Satan and sin. In Jesus name.

8.

Wherever you are--------------------- Receive encounter with Jesus right now. In the name of Jesus Christ.

9.

Because you ------------------- are connected to me and I believe in Christ and His Love, you are saved from sin to serve the living God through Christ Jesus. In Jesus name.

10.

Oh Lord my Father, I confess with Your Word, that every member of my household is saved to serve you. In Jesus name.

Chapter Five: Healing Prayers.

God's Promises.

1.

Heal me, O LORD, and I shall be healed; save me, and I shall be saved: for thou [art] my praise -

Jeremiah 17:14 -

2.

Who his own self bare our sins in his own body on the tree, that we, being dead to sins, should live unto righteousness: by whose stripes ye were healed - ***1 Peter 2:24*** *-*

3.

Behold, I will bring it health and cure, and I will cure them, and will reveal unto them the abundance of peace and truth - ***Jeremiah 33:6***

4.

But he [was] wounded for our transgressions, [he was] bruised for our iniquities: the chastisement of *our peace [was] upon him; and with his stripes we are healed. - **Isaiah 53:5***

5.

*Bless the LORD, O my soul, and forget not all his benefits: Who forgiveth all thine iniquities; who healeth all thy diseases; Who redeemeth thy life from destruction; who crowneth thee with lovingkindness and tender mercies - **Psalms 103:2-4** –*

6.

Is any sick among you? let him call for the elders of the church; and let them pray over him, anointing him with oil in the name of the Lord. And the prayer of faith shall save the sick, and the Lord shall raise him up; and if he have committed sins, they shall be forgiven him - **James 5:14-15**

7.

Beloved, I wish above all things that thou mayest prosper and be in health, even as thy soul prospereth - **3 John 1:2**

8.

And when he had called unto [him] his twelve disciples, he gave them power [against] unclean spirits, to cast them out, and to heal all manner of sickness and all manner of disease - **Matthew 10:1**

9.

And the LORD will take away from thee all sickness, and will put none of the evil diseases of Egypt, which thou knowest, upon thee; but will lay them upon all [them] that hate thee - **Deuteronomy 7:15**

Prayers & Declarations

1.

"Heavenly Father, it is Your will to heal us. It is Your will for us to walk in divine health. The price for our healing has been paid on the cross. Thank You Jesus.

2.

By the Blood of Jesus I claim forgiveness from any sin and disobedience causing this sickness in -------- ---------------------------in Jesus name.

3.

LORD, You forgive our sins and heal our diseases. Therefore I ask for forgiveness and total healing of this sickness in the life of---------------------in Jesus name.

4.

Every spirit that has caused this sickness in ------------------------------ I command you to get out this body and drown in abyss in Jesus name.

5.

Our bodies are the temple of the Holy Spirit. The bodies of my children are the temples of the Holy Spirit. Therefore, every spirit of defilement in ------------------, I cast you out right now. This body is not your home. I command you to go into abyss in Jesus name.

6.

As I anoint this body, I command a total restoration of health. My child ------------------ be healed in Jesus name.

7.

Let there be a Holy Ghost surgery in this body right now in Jesus name

---

8.

Holy Spirit, move into this body and restore every strength and health, In Jesus name.

9.

I decree that ------------------ will prosper and be in good health, even as the soul prospers in the Lord, in Jesus name.

10.

Thank You Jesus for our healing and divine health. Your work is permanent. Everything you do is perfect. Thank You Jesus.

Chapter Six: Prayers for Academic Excellence.

God's Promises

1. *"The LORD will make you the head, not the tail. If you pay attention to the commands of the LORD your God that I give you this day and carefully follow them, you will always be at the top, never at the bottom."* - **Deuteronomy 28:13:**

2.

"All your children will be taught by the LORD, and great will be their peace." - **Isaiah 54: 13:**

3.

I have more understanding than all my teachers: for thy testimonies [are] my meditation.- **Psalms 119:99**

4.

Forasmuch as an excellent spirit, and knowledge, and understanding, interpreting of dreams, and shewing of hard sentences, and dissolving of doubts, were found in the same Daniel, whom the king named Belteshazzar: now let Daniel be called, and he will shew the interpretation. **Daniel 5:12**

5.

"You are the light of the world. A city set on a hill cannot be hidden. Nor do people light a lamp and put it under a basket, but on a stand, and it gives light to all in the house. In the same way, let your light shine before others, so that they may see your good works and give glory to your Father who is in heaven." - **Matthew 5:14-16:**

6.

Then the king appointed Daniel to a high position and gave him many valuable gifts. He made Daniel ruler over the whole province of Babylon, as well as chief over all his wise men - **Daniel 2: 48:**

Prayers and Declarations.

1.

The Holy Spirit is the Spirit of excellence. Just like an excellent spirit was found in Joseph, Daniel and Jesus, Let ----------------- be empowered this moment with the spirit of excellence. In Jesus name.

2.

I decree that you will read and understand. You will hear and comprehend. And you will be the top in all that you do in school in Jesus name.

3.

While the teacher is teaching, God will be the one teaching you, and great shall be your peace, In Jesus name.

4.

You will have more understanding than your teachers, for the testimony of Christ is your strength, in Jesus name.

5.

O LORD, my Father, let ------------------- be a light wherever he is. Let his light so shine that men will be brought to your kingdom by his testimony, in Jesus name.

6.

I command every agent of darkness sent from the pit of hell to defile ------------------ to be disgraced in Jesus name.

7.

Every evil finger pointing at -------------------------- -be roasted by fire in Jesus name.

8.

The path of ------------------is as a shining light that will shine brighter and brighter, and no man or woman can extinguish it. In Jesus name.

9.

Every extinguisher of light, every destroyer of destiny, every tormenter, assigned against ------------------I command you to die by fire in Jesus name.

10.

My children are agents of light. They are bringers of good news and blessings. The power of God has given us all things that pertain unto life and godliness, through Jesus Christ. My children have escaped the corruption that is in this world through lust. In Jesus name. (2 Peter 1: 3-4)

Chapter Seven: Praying for the Prodigal, Disobedient Teen.

Our goal is not to condemn this child, but to stand in the gap and pray for God's intervention.

God's Promises.

1.

"But thus saith the LORD... I will contend with him that contendeth with thee, and I will save thy children." **Isaiah 49:25**:

2.

Behold, children are a gift of the LORD, The fruit of the womb is a reward. **Psalm 127:3-4**

3.

The king's heart is in the hand of the LORD, as the rivers of water: he turneth it whithersoever he will

*- **Proverbs 21:1***

4.

The blessing of the LORD, it maketh rich, and he addeth no sorrow with it. **Proverbs 10:22:**

5.

"Praise ye the LORD. Blessed is the man that feareth the LORD, that delighteth greatly in his commandments. His seed shall be mighty upon earth: the generation of the upright shall be blessed. " **Psalm 112:1 -2**

6.

"Verily I say unto you, Whatsoever ye shall bind on earth shall be bound in heaven: and whatsoever ye shall loose on earth shall be loosed in heaven."

Matthew 18: 18:

Prayers and Declarations

1.

Heavenly Father, I come to you in humility and ask you to forgive ---------for all kinds of unruly and rebellious behaviors in Jesus name.

---

2. I stand in the gap and pray that --------will not perish in Jesus name.

3.

LORD, reveal Yourself to -------------- in a very unique way. Cause him to encounter with Your power that will draw him to Your love and son, Jesus Christ. In Jesus name

---

4.

I ask the You turn the heart of------------- to your knowledge. In Jesus name.

5.

O LORD, You give us children to be a blessing to us and not to bring sorrows. I therefore come against every spirit of sorrow following -------- in Jesus name.

6.

Satan, I command you to loose your grips in the life of --------------- in the name of Jesus Christ.

7.

You spirits of rebellion. You spirits of lust. You spirits of anger, hate and bitterness. You spirits of greed, fear and waste. I bind all of you right now.

And I cast all of you out of ------------------- in Jesus name.

8.

For it is written, whatever I bind here on earth is bound in heaven and whatever i loose is loosed; I therefore loose --------------- and release him to the power of God in Jesus name.

9.

O LORD, arise and contend with those who are contending with me and my children, spiritually or physically, and save my children according to your Word, in Jesus name.

10.

From today LORD, the heart of--------------- is in your hand. He will live to your praise and glory, in Jesus name.

Chapter Eight: Prayers to Drive Away Fear, Discouragement and Depression in Children.

God's Promises.

1.

For God hath not given us the spirit of fear; but of power, and of love, and of a sound mind - **2 Timothy 1:7**

2.

Fear thou not; for I [am] with thee: be not dismayed; for I [am] thy God: I will strengthen thee; yea, I will help thee; yea, I will uphold thee with the right hand of my righteousness. **- Isaiah 41:10**

3.

I sought the LORD, and he heard me, and delivered me from all my fears. **- Psalms 34:4**

4.

For ye have not received the spirit of bondage again to fear; but ye have received the Spirit of adoption, whereby we cry, Abba, Father. -

Romans 8:15

5.

Thou shalt not be affrighted at them: for the LORD thy God [is] among you, a mighty God and terrible.

- Deuteronomy 7:21

6.

Have not I commanded thee? Be strong and of a good courage; be not afraid, neither be thou dismayed: for the LORD thy God [is] with thee whithersoever thou goest. - ***Joshua 1:9***

7.

"There is no fear in love; but perfect love casteth out fear: because fear hath torment. He that feareth is not made perfect in love." - ***1 John 4:8***

8.

But now thus saith the LORD that created thee, O Jacob, and he that formed thee, O Israel, Fear not:

for I have redeemed thee, I have called [thee] by thy name; thou [art] mine.

When thou passest through the waters, I [will be] with thee; and through the rivers, they shall not overflow thee: when thou walkest through the fire, thou shalt not be burned; neither shall the flame kindle upon thee. - **Isaiah 43: 1-2**

Prayers & Prophetic Declarations.

1.

O LORD, You have not given us the spirit of fear, but of power, of love and of a sound mind. I therefore command the spirit of fear and depression to get out of ---------------right now, in Jesus name.

2.

Heavenly Father, deliver --------------from all his fears and show Him the magnitude of Your power with Him, in Jesus name.

3.

As the LORD has said in Joshua 1:9 ----------------- you'll be strong and of a good courage; you'll not be afraid or dismayed: for the LORD thy God is with thee wherever you go, in Jesus name.

4.

In Isaiah 54:4 God says ------------------you should not be afraid because you will not be put to shame; you will not be disgraced; you will not be humiliated. In Jesus name.

5.

O LORD, I present ---------------------to You. You said in Matthew 11:28, let those who are heavy *laden come to you, that You'll give them rest. O LORD, Give -------------------------rest, in Jesus name.*

6.

Whatever is making -----------------------to be depressed, discouraged and fearful, I command them to be rolled away this moment, in Jesus name.

7.

Holy Spirit, restore the joy of the Lord in------------- ------------in the name of Jesus Christ.

8.

From today, I decree that --------------------shall be bold, strong and joyful. In Jesus name.

9.

Because the LORD is for us, no one can be against us, in Jesus name. No one can be against------------ ------in Jesus name.

10.

I decree, according to the WORD or the LORD in Deuteronomy 28:6: Your going out shall be a blessing and your coming back shall be a blessing, in Jesus name.

Chapter Nine: Prayers for Guidance in Choosing Career and Relationship.

God's Promises.

1.

Trust in the LORD with all thine heart; and lean not unto thine own understanding. In all thy ways acknowledge him, and he shall direct thy paths. -

Proverbs 3:5-6

2.

I will instruct thee and teach thee in the way which thou shalt go: I will guide thee with mine eye. - **Psalms 32:8.**

3.

And thine ears shall hear a word behind thee, saying, This [is] the way, walk ye in it, when ye turn to the right hand, and when ye turn to the left. **- Isaiah 30:21.**

4.

But the Comforter, [which is] the Holy Ghost, whom the Father will send in my name, he shall teach you all things, and bring all things to your remembrance, whatsoever I have said unto you. - **John 14:26**

5.

If any of you lack wisdom, let him ask of God, that giveth to all [men] liberally, and upbraideth not; and it shall be given him. - **James 1:5**

6.

The meek will he guide in judgment: and the meek will he teach his way. - **Psalms 25:9-10**

Prayers and Prophetic Declarations.

1.

O LORD, by strength shall no man prevail. I come to you in humility and ask for Your guidance for ------------------, in the name of Jesus Christ.

2.

Holy Spirit, the greatest teacher, teach --------------- -----------in the way that he should go in his career and relationship, in Jesus name.

3.

Every snare of the devil against--------------------in his relationship and career plan, I destroy them today in Jesus name.

4.

O LORD my Father, I pray this day that ------------- ------------will make the right choice in his career and relationship in Jesus name.

5.

Any man or woman sent by the devil to distract and cause ---------------- to deviate from God's career and relationship plan, LORD, I command such men and women to be disgraced and banished in Jesus name.

6.

I decree that ---------------will walk in the path ordained for him by God, in his career and relationship, in Jesus name.

7.

Even though the horse is prepared against the day of battle, victory and safety is of the LORD (Proverbs 21:31). -------------------will have victory and be safe at all times in Jesus name.

8.

LORD, grant ----------------victory and safety in his career and relationship. In Jesus name.

9.

Give------------------wisdom to make the right decisions at all times in his career and relationship, in Jesus name.

10.

Give him strength to be firm in judgment and righteousness in Jesus name.

Chapter Ten: Prayers for Protection.

God's Promises.

1.

Psalm 91 is a very powerful protection scripture and prayer. Below, I have adapted it for you to pray for divine protection over anyone, your children, your family, etc.

2.

But the Lord is faithful, who shall establish you, and keep you from evil. - **2 Thessalonians 3:3**

3.

And the Lord shall deliver me from every evil work, and will preserve [me] unto his heavenly kingdom: to whom [be] glory for ever and ever. Amen. - **2 Timothy 4:18**

Prayers And Prophetic Declarations:

1.

Because we dwell in the secret place of the most High, we shall abide under the shadow of the Almighty. In Jesus name.

2.

I will say of the LORD, He is my refuge and my fortress: my God; in him will I trust. Surely he shall deliver ------------- from the snare of the fowler, and from the noisome pestilence. In Jesus name.

3.

God will cover ------------ with his feathers, and under his wings shall he. God's truth shall be his shield and buckler. In Jesus name.

5.

You shall not be afraid for the terror by night; nor for the arrow that flies by day; Nor for the pestilence that walks in darkness; nor for the destruction that happens in the afternoon.

6.

A thousand shall fall at your side, and ten thousand at your right hand; but it shall not come near you. In Jesus name.

7.

Because ------------------has made the LORD his refuge and fortress, only with his eyes shall he behold and see the reward of the wicked. There shall no evil befall him, neither shall any disease come near his house. In Jesus name.

8.

God will give his angels charge over ---------------- to keep you in all your ways. They shall bear you up in [their] hands; you will not dash your foot against a stone. In Jesus name.

9.

You shall tread upon the lion and serpent: You will trample the dragons under your feet. In Jesus name.

10.

God will deliver ------------ and set him on high and satisfy him with long life, in Jesus name.

ADAPTED FROM PSAL 91.

Chapter Eleven: General Prayers and Declarations For Your Children.

This kind of prayers can be made every day, joined with any specific prayer points above.

1.

Children are gifts from the LORD. The gifts of God only bring riches, and add no sorrow with them. (Psalm 127:3, Prov. 10:22).

I decree therefore that my children shall only bring me riches, peace and prosperity. I shall not have cause for sorrow from the

children that God has blessed me with, In Jesus name.

2.

The heart of a king is in the hand of God and He turns it wherever He pleases (Prov. 21:1)

Therefore I decree that the hearts of my children are turned to the Lord, in Jesus name.

I decree that ....is turned to the LORD and following the service of God in Jesus name.

3.

My children shall be taught of the LORD God Almighty, and great shall be their peace. (Isaiah 54:13).

So I decree today that my children shall have peace. They shall excel and be the head in all that they do, in Jesus name.

4.

This is what the LORD says: Even the captives of the mighty shall be taken away, and the prey of the terrible shall be delivered: for I will contend with him that contendeth with thee, and I will save thy children.(Isaiah 49:25)

Heavenly Father, contend with everyone that is contending with my family and save my children (mention names) according to Your Word, In Jesus name.

5.

Jesus said, "your Father in heaven is not willing that any of these little ones should perish."

(Matthew 18:14)

My children will not perish. They are saved and serving the LORD in Jesus name.

Other Books from the Same Publisher.

1. <u>200 Violent Prayers</u> for Deliverance, Healing and Financial Breakthrough.

2. <u>GRIEF AND LOSS:</u> Hearing God's Voice in Painful Moments: 21 Days Bible Meditations and Prayers to Bring Comfort, Strength and Healing When Grieving for the Loss of Someone You Love.

3. <u>Healing Prayers:</u> 30 Powerful Prophetic Prayers that Brings Healing and Empower You to Walk in Divine Health.

4. <u>Healing WORDS:</u> 55 Powerful Daily Confessions & Declarations to Activate Your Healing & Walk in Divine Health: Strong Decrees That Invoke Healing for You & Your Loved Ones

5. <u>Prayers That Break Curses and Spells and Release Favors and Breakthroughs.</u>

6. [7 Days Fasting With 120 Powerful Night Prayers for Personal Deliverance and Breakthrough.](#)

7. [100 Powerful Prayers for Teenagers](#)

8. [How to Pray for Your Children Every Day.](#)

9. [How to Pray for Your Family:](#) + 70 Powerful Prayers and Prophetic Declarations for Your Family's Salvation, Healing, Victory, Breakthrough & Total Restoration.

10. [Daily Prayer Guide:](#) A Practical Guide to Praying and Getting Results – Learn How to Develop a Powerful Personal Prayer Life

11. [Make Him Respect You:](#) 31 Relationship Advice for Women to Make their Men Respect Them.

12. [How to Cleanse Your Home and Property from Demonic Attacks](#)

13. <u>Praying Through the Book of Psalms:</u> Discover Great Psalms, Powerful Prayers & Declarations for Every Situation: Birthday, Christmas, Business Ideas, Breakthrough, Deliverance, Healing, Comfort, Exams, Decision Making, Grief, and Many More.

Talk to Us.

Thank you for reading this book. I believe you have been blessed.

Please consider giving this book a review on Amazon.

I also invite you to checkout our website at www.BetterLifeWorld.org and consider joining our newsletter, which we send out once in a while with great tips, testimonies and revelations from God's Word for a victorious living.

Feel free to drop us your prayer request. We will join faith with you and God's power will be released in your life and the issue in question.

About the Author.

Katie Armstrong is a pastor's wife, school teacher and prayer leader. She has a degree in Medical Physiology and a background as a registered child care professional. Over the years, Katie has seen the effect of prayers on children and families. She encourages parents to spend time and pray for their children and homes with the scriptures and believe God for breakthroughs in life.

She is the women leader and prayer coordinator at Better Life World Outreach Center (www.betterlifeworld.org). She speaks on a variety of subjects like prayer, fasting, food, home care, social media and raising Godly children.

If you want a humble prayer partner and guide, then Katie is your person

Made in the USA
San Bernardino, CA
17 October 2017